All About Austr

100+ Fascinating Fun Facts & Trivia

By Bandana Ojha

Introduction

Filled with up-to-date information, color photos, fascinating & fun facts this book " All About Australia: 100+ Fascinating Fun Facts & Trivia" is the best book for kids as well the entire family to find out more about the world's biggest island but the smallest continent. This book would satisfy the children's curiosity and help them to understand why Australia is special—and what makes it different from other country. This book gives a story, history, the official symbols, how Australia got her name, people, places and many more. It is a fun way for young readers to find out more interesting and fun facts of Oceania. This is a great chance for every kid as well as the entire family to expand their knowledge about one of the best-educated and wealthiest nation and impress their friends with all "discovered and never knew before" amazing and interesting fun facts.

1. Australia is a continent surrounded by the Indian Ocean and the Pacific Ocean.

2. Australia/Oceania is the smallest continent of the seven continents.

3. The country is divided into six states: Southern Australia, Western Australia, New South Wales, Queensland, Victoria, and

Tasmania and two self-governing territories: Northern Territory and Australian Capital Territory.

4. Due to its large size and isolation from the rest of the world, Australia is sometimes known as the 'island continent'.

5. Australia is the sixth largest country in the world, after Russia, Canada, USA, China, and Brazil.

6. Human habitation of the Australian continent is known to have begun at least 65,000 years ago with the migration of people called the aboriginal people of Australia.

7. Chinese explorers travelled to Australia long before Europeans arrived. As early as the 1400s, sailors and fisherman came to

Australia for sea-cucumbers and to trade with Indigenous peoples.

8. The first European to visit Australia was Dutch explorer Willem Janszoon, in 1606. More Dutch explorers visited the country over the next hundred years, plotting maps and naming it 'New Holland'.

9. The name Australia was given to the country in 1824. It comes from the word 'terra australis incognita' that means 'unknown southern island'.

10. British began to settle there in 1788.

11. 91% of the country is covered by native vegetation.

12. Australia is 10th richest country in the world with gross domestic product (GDP) per capita) $58,824.

13. Australia is ranked second on the Human Development Index based on life expectancy, income, and education.

14. Australia is a megadiverse country, its size gives it a wide variety of landscapes, with deserts in the center, tropical rainforests in the north-east, and mountain ranges in the south-east.

15. The current population of Australia is over 25 M.

16. There are about 3 people per square mile.

17. A person from Australia is called Aussie.

18. The Australian way of saying 'hello' is G'day.

19. Canberra is the capital city of Australia.

20. Canberra is located at the northern end of the Australian Capital Territory; 170 mi south-west of Sydney and 410 mi north-east of Melbourne.

21. The word "Canberra" is popularly claimed to derive from the word Kambera or Canberry, which is claimed to mean "meeting place" in Ngunnawal, one of the Indigenous languages spoken by Aboriginal people.

22. Melbourne was the capital city of Australia for 26 years between 1901 and 1927 before the capital shifted to Canberra.

23. The flag of Australia is the official national flag of Australia.

24. The Australian flag uses three prominent symbols: The Union Flag, the Commonwealth Star and the Southern Cross.

25. The flag's original design with a six-pointed Commonwealth Star was chosen in 1901 from entries in a competition held following Federation and was first flown in Melbourne on 3 September 1901.

26. September 3rd is the Australian National Flag Day.

27. January 26th is the National Day of Australia.

28. National Day of Australia takes place every year and is a celebration of different cultures, races, religions, beliefs, and views.

29. The date is the anniversary of the unfurling of the British flag at Sydney Cove in 1788.

30. The Golden Wattle was proclaimed the national floral emblem in August 1988.

31. There are more than 760 different types of wattle across Australia.

32. The Golden Wattle is a symbol of unity.

33. Kangaroos and emus cannot walk backward, one of the reasons that they are on the Australian coat of arms.

34. The Australian coat of arms consists of a shield containing the badges of the six Australian states symbolizing federation, and the national symbols of the Golden Wattle, the kangaroo, and the emu.

35. The national animal of Australia is Red
Kangaroo.

36. It is the largest terrestrial mammal endemic to Australia and is found across the mainland. Their total population is almost double the human population of Australia.

37. There are over 60 different species of kangaroos in Australia.

38. Australian airline Qantas uses a kangaroo as their symbol.

39. Kangaroo meat can be purchased from the supermarket and is known to be a leaner and healthier alternative to beef or lamb with a 1-2 percent fat content.

40. "Advance Australia Fair" is the national anthem of Australia.

41. The national bird of Australia is Emu.

42. Australia has no national fruit. Australia has large-scale fruit production consists mainly of pears, apples, grapes, and cherries. They supply huge amount of fruits every year.

43. There are as many as 400 wild cherry trees growing in many regions in Australia.

44. Australia is considered the number one wine producer around the world. more than 7 billion bottles of wine are produced by the country.

45. Australia has over 60 separate wine regions.

46. The Australian War Memorial is a national memorial remembering all armed forces and groups who have died or entered in the wars of the Commonwealth of

Australia. The Australian War Memorial is in Canberra, capital of Australia.

47. The national colors of Australia are green and gold.

48. National gemstone of Australia is Opal.

49. The highest point of Australia is Mount Kosciuszko with 2.228metres or 7,310ft.

50. Mount Townsend is the second highest mountain in Australia's Mainland with a height of 7,247 feet, only 2.3 miles less than the highest mountain, Kosciuszko.

51. Mount Twynam is the third highest mountain in Australia's mainland with an elevation of 7,201 feet. It is located five miles north-east of Mount Kosciuszko.

52. Australia has 516 national parks to protect its unique plants and animals.

53. Lake Eyre officially known as Kati Thanda is the lowest natural point in Australia, at approximately 15 m (49 ft) below sea level.

54. The longest river of Australia is the Murray River with 2,508km/1558 miles.

55. More than 85% of Australians live within 50km of the coast.

56. There are more than 10,000 beaches across the country.

57. One million wild camels roam over the Australian deserts. They were originally brought to help with railroad construction.

58. Australia includes the world's longest stretch of dead-straight railway track, a 297 miles length.

59. Australia has 19 world heritage listed sites including historic townships, cities, and landscapes.

60. Sydney is the state capital of New South Wales and the most populous city in Australia.

61. It is one of the most multicultural cities in the world. More than 250 different languages are spoken in Sydney.

62. Sydney has the third-largest foreign-born population of any city in the world after London and New York City.

63. 33% of Australians were born in another country

64. Over 300 different languages and dialects are spoken in Australia including 45 Indigenous languages.

65. 21% of Australians do not speak English at home.

66. The longest fence in the world is in Australia, and it runs for over 5,530 kilometers.

67. Despite being one of the most expensive cities in the world, Sydney frequently ranks in the top ten most livable cities in the world.

68 The iconic Opera House was opened in 1973 and was designed by Danish architect Jørn Utzon. This is one of the world's most famous landmarks.

69. Highway 1 in Australia is the longest highway in the world, spanning around 9,000 miles in total.

70. In 1902, women received the right to vote in Australia. This made the country the second in the world to implement this. (New Zealand was first).

71. Fraser Island is the largest sand island in the world.

72. Nullarbor Links measuring more than 850 miles,18-hole par 72 golf course, said to be "the World's Longest Golf course" is in Australia.

73. After China, the largest number of sheep can be found in Australia. There are approximately 100 million of sheep across the country. That is why Australia is one of the world's leading producers of wool.

74. The World Surfing Championship was first held in Sydney, Australia, during 1964.

75. Australia is the only continent which does not have an active volcano.

76. Melbourne is considered the sporting capital of the world, as it has more top-level sport available for its citizens than anywhere else.

77. Melbourne has the world's largest Greek population outside of Athens.

78. Melbourne has the highest number of restaurants and cafes per number of people than any other city in the world.

79. Melbourne's Luna Park is the oldest privately-owned theme park in the world.

80. Tasmania has the cleanest air in the world.

81. The Great Barrier Reef in Eastern Australia consists of more than 3,000 reefs in which live more than 350 species of corals and over 1,500 species of fish.

82. It is the biggest coral reef in the world.

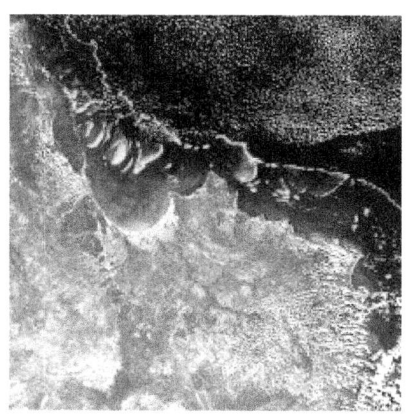

83. The world's first compulsory seat belt law was put into place in Victoria in 1970.

84. The Great Victoria Desert, just ONE of Australia's barren areas is larger than the United Kingdom.

85. A single cattle ranch in South Australia is larger than the state of Israel.

86. The only two mammals in the world that lay eggs are found in Australia, the platypus and echidna.

87. Australia produces more than 1 million tons of apples in year.

88. Ayers Rock also called 'Uluru' which is in the center of the country is the largest alone standing rock in the world.

89. Road signs in Australia warn drivers about kangaroos that might hop across the roads.

90. Australia has over 750 different reptile species, more than any other country in the world.

91. There are 36 species of poisonous funnel-web spiders and 20 types of venomous snakes are there in Australia.

92. The Australian Alps get more snow than the Swiss Alps.

93. Australia holds the Guinness World Record for the most amount of Christmas lights on a house - over half a million.

92.

94. There are only 25 venomous snakes in the world and Australia has 20 of them.

95. Australia is the world's largest exporter of coal.

96. Although it is rich in natural resources and has a lot of fertile land, more than one-third of Australia is desert.

97. Australia is driest inhabited continent of the world.

98. The highest temperature ever reached in Australia was 123.26 degrees Fahrenheit (50.7 degrees Celsius).

99. The lowest temperature was minus 73 degrees Fahrenheit

(-58.33 degrees Celsius).

100. Boomerang, a wooden weapon used for hunting which returns to its thrower, invented by the Aboriginal people of Australia.

101. Sydney is the highest-ranking city in the world for international students.

102. More than 50,000 international student study at the city's universities and a further 50,000 study at its vocational and English language schools.

103. Melbourne has been referred to as "the live music capital of the world". It has more music venues per capital than any other city

Please check this out:

Our other best-selling books for kids are-

All About **New York**: 100+ Amazing Facts with Pictures

All About **New Jersey**: 100+ Amazing Facts with Pictures

All About **California**: 100+ Amazing Facts with Pictures

All About **Arizona**: 100+ Amazing Facts with Pictures

All About **Massachusetts**: 100+ Amazing Facts with Pictures

All About **Minnesota**: 100+ Amazing Facts with Pictures

All About **Florida**: 100+ Amazing Facts with Pictures

All About **Texas**: 100+ Amazing Facts with Pictures

All About **Italy**: 100+ Amazing Facts with Pictures

Know about **Sharks**: 100 Amazing Fun Facts with Pictures

Know About **Whales**:100+ Amazing & Interesting Fun Facts with Pictures

Know About Dinosaurs: 100 Amazing & Interesting Fun Facts with Pictures

Know About Kangaroos: Amazing & Interesting Facts with Pictures

Know About Penguins: 100+ Amazing Penguin Facts with Pictures

Know About Dolphins :100 Amazing Dolphin Facts with Pictures

Know About Elephant

Most Popular Animal Quiz book for Kids: 100 amazing animal facts

Quiz Book for Kids: Science, History, Geography, Biology, Computer & Information Technology

English Grammar for Kids: Most Easy Way to learn English Grammar

Solar System & Space Science- Quiz for Kids: What You Know About Solar System

100 Amazing Quiz Q & A About Penguin: Never Known Before Penguin Facts

English Grammar Practice Book for elementary kids: 1000+ Practice Questions with Answers

A to Z of English Tense

Printed in Great Britain
by Amazon

12969606R00031